The Easter Story

Story adaptation by
Sarah Toast

Illustrations by
Thomas Gianni

Louis Weber, C.E.O.
Publications International, Ltd.
7373 North Cicero Avenue
Lincolnwood, Illinois 60712

www.pubint.com

Manufactured in China.

8 7 6 5 4 3 2 1

ISBN: 0-7853-7852-9

When Jesus died, a follower asked the Roman governor, Pontius Pilate, for the body. Joseph of Arimathea wrapped the body in linen cloth. He laid Jesus' body in a new tomb that was cut out of rock. Then a heavy stone was rolled across the opening of the burial cave.

Jesus had said, "After three days, I will rise again." Pilate was afraid that someone would take the body and then pretend that Jesus had been raised from the dead, so he sent Roman guards to watch the tomb.

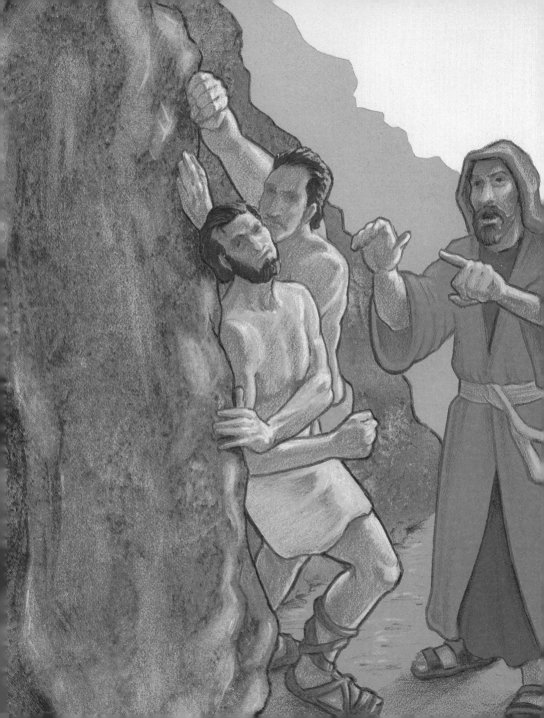

Jesus had been buried on the Friday of his death. Very early in the morning, on the Sunday after he died, an angel of the Lord appeared.

The angel, who arrived at the tomb of Jesus, was a young man dressed in a shining robe. The angel easily rolled the huge stone away from the mouth of Jesus' tomb. Then he went and sat in the tomb.

The Roman guards were astonished and filled with fear at this sight. They fainted from terror.

Not long after, three women stopped by the tomb to put sweet-smelling spices on Jesus' body. They had planned to ask for help moving the stone.

When they arrived, the women saw the stone had already been moved from the tomb. Then they saw the angel.

The angel said, "Jesus is not here. He has risen, just as he said he would. Go now, and tell his followers that Jesus has been raised from the dead."

The women left to find Jesus' other followers.

When they returned, the women told Jesus' disciples about the tomb and the angel. Most of them thought that the women were making a mistake.

Peter and John ran to the tomb to see for themselves what had happened. There they saw the cloth strips that had been wrapped around Jesus' body, but Jesus was not there. They saw that the tomb was empty and believed that Jesus had come back to life.

Quickly, the two returned to tell the other disciples.

Meanwhile, some Roman guards had made their way back to the city and told their leaders what had happened at the tomb. The leaders gathered together and quickly thought up a plan to keep the people from finding out that Jesus had risen from the dead.

They collected a large sum of money and promised to give it to the guards if they would tell a lie. The guards agreed to say that Jesus' followers had come in the night and stolen his body while they were asleep.

Later that day, two of Jesus' followers were talking about what had happened.

Another man came along and walked with them. It was Jesus, but the men did not recognize him.

Jesus asked what the two men were talking about. One of the men sadly told about the death of Jesus. He told about how some women from their group had gone to his empty tomb and were told by an angel that Jesus had risen. He told about how Peter and John had also seen the empty tomb.

Then the unknown man explained to the two that Jesus had to suffer death and then rise from the dead, as all the prophets had foretold. Still the men did not recognize Jesus.

It was getting late when they came near their village, so the two men urged their new friend to stay with them for the night. While they were eating their supper, Jesus blessed the bread and broke it, then gave it to them. Suddenly the two men recognized Jesus, but just as suddenly he disappeared.

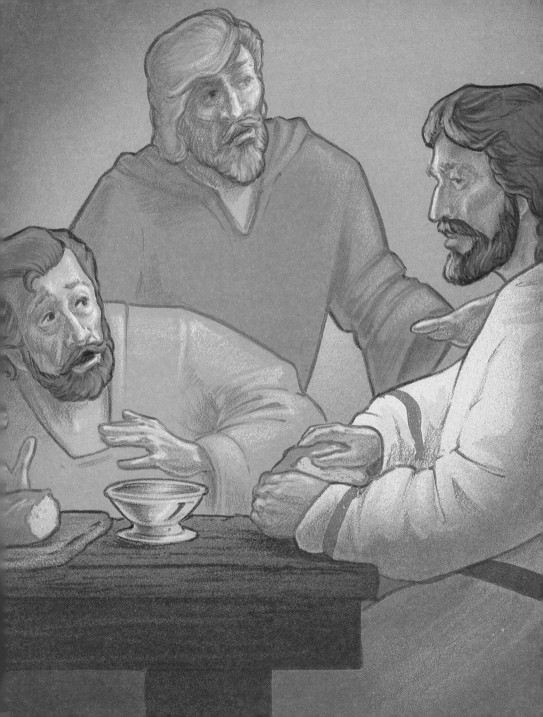

The two men hurried off to Jerusalem to find Jesus' disciples. They told them of how they had talked with Jesus and had recognized him when he broke the bread.

Suddenly Jesus was with the disciples saying, "Peace be with you." All of his followers were thrilled.

But there was one disciple who was not there. Thomas wouldn't believe that his friends had been with Jesus until he could see him for himself.

A week later Jesus appeared when Thomas was there. Now he believed!

Some weeks later, Jesus again met with his eleven disciples. He spoke on a hill in Galilee called the Mount of Olives. There Jesus told them, "I have work for you to do. Go to people everywhere and teach what I have taught you. And do not forget, I am with you always, until the end of time."

When he had just finished saying this, Jesus raised his hands to bless all of the disciples. As he did so, Jesus was lifted up to Heaven until a cloud hid him from the view of the disciples.

The disciples all gazed up. Then two men in white robes stood with them. They said, "Why do you stand looking up toward Heaven? Jesus will come back some day just as he went to Heaven."

Then the disciples all went out and began to teach about Jesus.